The Art of Worship

The Art of Worship

EVERY PICTURE TELLS A STORY AND EVERY STORY CREATES A PICTURE

We Will Be Like Trees Planted by the Rivers of Water

Angela Patterson

XULON PRESS

Xulon Press
2301 Lucien Way #415
Maitland, FL 32751
407.339.4217
www.xulonpress.com

Paperback ISBN-13: 978-1-6628-3977-1
Hard Cover ISBN-13: 978-1-6628-3978-8
Ebook ISBN-13: 978-1-6628-3979-5

Dedication

To all those people who have invested in my life by mentoring me,
speaking words of life into my life, teaching me, and pouring into me.

To all my family whom I hold dear to my heart and especially to my mom, Kathy,
who is my best friend, my sister in Christ, and my prayer partner,
and to my children who cheered on my amateur artwork and loved me through my shortcomings.

To all my sisters in Christ who pray with me and for me on a regular basis.
To a few that I feel compelled to name by name
because of the profound impact they have had in my life and spiritual journey:
Wanda, Karen, Susan, Becky, Rachel, Megan, Cindy, Geralyn, Judy, Luci,
and especially Carolyn, who has prayed for countless hours with me and for me.

To my home church for many years, Crooked Creek Baptist Church,
where God grew me, nurtured me, and prepared me for even more that was still to come,
and to Pastor Brenson Jennings for his great heart of compassion for people and souls.

To my current church home, Living Hope Church,
where I met the Holy Spirit in relationship and fell in love with worship and intimacy with God.
To Pastor David Holt and to all Living Hope Church leadership, including the worship team
and the prayer ministry team.

To my husband, Dino, whom I love with all my heart.

Special thanks to:

Lucius and Jennifer Malcolm who read many of my journal entries and offered feedback.

Judy Childs for speaking words of life into my life and giving me vision beyond my limitations.

Cindy Mackey for teaching and mentoring me and connecting my heart to the
Father's heart in a deeper way.

Dr. David Holt for messages of truth and grace that have impacted my spiritual growth.

Patti Smith who helped with editing and ideas.

Kathy Hoyt who helped with proofreading.

Mary Kathryn Suplita who suggested creating a coffee table book in the first place,

and especially to Holy Spirit, Our Lord Jesus Christ, and Heavenly Father—our great Triune God!

Table of Contents

Preface

My Journey to Worship

For a long time, I did not know worship was more than just singing hymns out of a hymn book to God the Father. Maybe I did know, but there can be a difference in knowing and really knowing. I am sure I knew in my head worship included prayer and even singing spontaneous songs to God while driving in the car or singing in the shower, but there is a depth to worship far beyond anything I had ever known intellectually or had ever experienced.

Then God, as He sometimes does, picked me up and put me in a place I did not choose because He was about to reveal to me aspects of worship that cannot be taught from the written page. He put me in a place where I would experience worship corporately with a body of believers, and I would experience it individually in my own spirit. These experiences of worship would come in many forms to my surprised and hungry heart.

I had always shied away from the word *experience* when it came in conjunction with my faith. Somehow, I had come to believe the idea that religious experiences were not valid and maybe not even good. Then as God began to open my heart to worship, the Holy Spirit began to reveal truths to my heart that I had formerly been closed to. He showed me that knowing someone meant being in relationship with them, and

a relationship is an experience. God wanted me to experience Him. He desired to draw me into a relationship with Him so that I might know Him in experience instead of just knowing about Him. The more I knew Him, the more I desired to worship Him.

My communication with God the Father, God the Son, and God the Holy Spirit changed dramatically as I entered into this new relationship with our great Triune God. Jesus became the focal point in my heart, and I met the Holy Spirit in relationship. I moved from a head knowledge to a genuine heart-knowing during conversational prayer and two-way journaling. I began to write what I felt my Father spoke to me by the promptings of His indwelling Spirit. This new heart-knowing changed everything. It was not long after I learned to experience God through His written Word, through music, through messages, through expressions like raised hands, through the two-way journaling, and through being in fellowship with other believers that the pictures in my heart began to flow.

This book documents the artistic side of my journey into worshiping on God's great dance floor—the stage on which I found myself with people from many tribes, tongues, and languages, all with a heart to follow Christ and worship our King. This book also draws from many of my two-way journal entries. I treasure God's words to me but always carefully compare them to His infallible written Word, which is my absolute standard for truth.

Because I am human and I am fallible, I realize I can make mistakes even in my hearing from God and my two-way journaling. Therefore, all that I share in this book or any book is simply my sharing what I believe God spoke to me personally. In no way do I put these journal entries on the level with Scripture or declare they are a thus-saith-the-Lord proclamation. They are simply His love letters to me, His beloved daughter.

Holy, Holy, Holy is the Lord God Almighty

After watching a talented artist demonstrate beautiful prophetic painting during a church service, something stirred and then yearned deep within my own heart. I came home that day and picked up a paintbrush for the first time to paint with acrylic paints on canvas. I had never seen art brought forth as an act of worship. I had enjoyed a little art years ago with pastels on paper, but I had never known art could actually be an act of worship. With no formal training and no knowledge of techniques, I watched a couple of YouTube videos on how to mix colors and apply acrylic paints onto canvas. Then I jumped right in.

It is humbling to include my first messy attempts at painting and even more humbling to include my first attempts at lettering, but my heart was worshiping as the paint and the words took form on the canvas. My love for God, my awe for Him, and my deep desire to express my heart found joy even in the amateur attempts to paint. Who could have known that painting could be an act of worship! Very quickly I found that a message in the form of words flowed with each picture. Sometimes the pictures came first and sometimes the words, but in every case one would write the other. It no longer mattered that each attempt was amateur and childish. The worship that flowed with the paintings made it worth it all.

The journal entry that prompted this painting came from a homework assignment in a Transformational Discipleship class at my church. This entry was written on September 10, 2019.

"There are times in life that the darkness of sin, of storms, of pain, or of the attacks of the enemy hide God from our human sight. But in those times as we turn to Him in repentance and dependence, He gives us spiritual sight to see beyond the darkness. And yet, we cannot approach Him because He is perfect and holy and pure; yet, we can approach Him because we are wrapped in the perfect pure holiness of Christ's robes of righteousness. And as we approach Him, we approach Him in praise and in worship, and all His works praise Him with us.

When I first learned to hear God's voice to me and to become aware of His great love for me and to see Him as my Heavenly Father, like a perfect loving daddy, His holiness overpowered my ability to view Him like a daddy to me. His holiness made me doubt my ability to talk to Him as a friend talks to a friend. I felt it was almost sacrilegious for me to consider myself involved in a conversation with Him where His answers to me were not begged for, sought for, looked for, searched for—instead they were just listened for. I knew He spoke through His written Word, through sermons, books, messages, and songs—but for Him to speak to me was almost more than I could accept. As I journaled out my concern even of this to Him, He spoke to me and assured me that my knowing Him in the intimacy of a friend-to-friend relationship in no way diminished His holiness. This mystery was almost as great a mystery as the Trinity or the mystery of predestination in harmony with free will—that I, a sinful human, could know in relationship and could fellowship with a holy God. This mystery highlighted the cross and Jesus's death and resurrection. To know—not in facts or black and white words on a page—but to know the meaning of invitation to be in God's presence because of Christ's robes of righteousness causes me to cry with the song writer, holy, holy, holy.

There have been times, especially as I listened to the entire book of Genesis in one sitting, in which God's awesome holiness would overwhelm me so greatly I almost could not continue listening because His holiness so highlights my sinfulness. But through Christ and His righteousness I can stay there in His Word. Only Christ!"

Isaiah 6:3
Holy, holy, holy,
is the Lord of hosts:
the whole earth *is* full of His glory.

Revelation 4:8
Holy, holy, holy, Lord God Almighty,
which was, and is, and is to come.

The Holiness of God

How Deep the Father's Love for Us

My second attempt to paint as an act of worship came the following week as I completed another homework assignment in the same Transformational Discipleship class. For the *Going Deeper* section of the homework, we were to draw a picture, write a poem, or write a song about God's love. Immediately the Lord reminded me of a song He had given me in August 2017. Because I have no musical training and only sing when I am alone, I had voice recorded the song on my phone to keep from forgetting the words and tune.

Going out on an embarrassing limb, I sent the voice recording to a real musician and asked her if she could take the poem and make a real song from it. She added a chorus and adjusted some of the words and created a beautiful song, including adding real music.

God's Love

I will never forget the first time I heard her sing it when she sent her own video recording to me. I wept as the words and melody lifted my heart right up to heaven. I had never tasted worship in this form either. Worship was and still is a treasure that comes from being awed and overwhelmed by the love and presence of God.

Psalm 92:50
Lord, how great are thy works!
and Thy thoughts are very deep

Jeremiah 31:3
Yea, I have loved thee
with an everlasting love:
therefore with lovingkindness
have I drawn thee.

I stand amazed at Your presence, Lord
I stand amazed at Your holiness
I stand amazed at Your awesome power
I stand amazed at who You are and who I am
I'm a child of the King,
a child of the King I stand amazed

I sing Your praises for Your goodness, Lord
I sing Your praises for Your righteousness
I sing Your praises for Your beauty, Lord
I sing Your praises for who You are and who I am
I'm a child of the King
a child of the King I sing Your praise

I bow the knee at Your sovereignty
I bow the knee at Your perfect will
I bow the knee at Your Deity
I bow the knee at who You are and who I am
I'm a child of the King
a child of the King I bow the knee

I stand amazed at Your love, oh Lord
I stand amazed at Your sacrifice
I stand amazed at the cross of Christ
I stand amazed at who You are and who I am
I'm a child of the King
a child of the King I stand amazed

Original Poem from August 2017
4th verse added for homework assignment in 2019

I Stand Amazed (Megan Hodgson Southwick)

Verse 1:
I stand amazed at Your presence, Lord
I stand amazed at Your holiness
I stand amazed at Your awesome power
I stand amazed at who You are and who I am

Verse 2
I sing Your praises for Your goodness, Lord
I sing Your praises for Your righteousness
I sing Your praises for Your beauty, Lord
I sing Your praises for who You are and who I am

Pre-chorus:
I'm a child of the King

Chorus:
Here I stand in the wake of Your glory
Here I stand in Your grace
Jesus Savior, I will follow
Nothing compares, nothing compares to Your love

Verse 3:
I bow the knee at Your sovereignty
I bow the knee at Your perfect will
I bow the knee at Your Deity
I bow the knee at who You are and who I am

Pre-chorus:
I'm a child of the King

Chorus:
Here I stand in the wake of Your glory
Here I stand in Your grace
Jesus Savior, I will follow
Nothing compares, nothing compares to Your love

Verse 4:
I stand amazed at Your love, oh Lord
I stand amazed at Your sacrifice
I stand amazed at the cross of Christ
I stand amazed at who You are and who I am

Pre-chorus:
I'm a child of the King

Chorus:
Here I stand in the wake of Your glory
Here I stand in Your grace
Jesus Savior, I will follow
Nothing compares, nothing compares to Your love

A Harvest of Souls

2 Timothy 2:6
The husbandman that laboureth must be first partaker of the fruits.

My third painting came as a result of another homework assignment in another Transformational Discipleship class. One of the questions referenced 2 Timothy 2:2–7 as this passage speaks about the soldier, the athlete, and the farmer. The question went on to ask which of the three examples spoke to me most. I wrote the following for my answer:

The farmer analogy spoke to me. I love gardening and growing things, and I love the laws of the harvest. They give me a deep sense of hope for those I have poured into the deepest—my children. Why? Because a harvest is not dependent on my skill as much as it is dependent on God and His perfect Word. A harvest is dependent on the condition of the ground, which corresponds to the heart of the recipient. The skill of the sower is not so much the issue as is his or her obedience to scatter the seed and then be faithful to water, to weed, and to tend the crop. Where I failed, God's Word never fails. We reap what we sow. We reap more than we sow. We reap in a different season than we sow.

Let the hard things in life drive us into God, and in that secret place with Him let us ask for a passion and a filling of His Spirit. As His filling creates a passion within us, let us all ask God for the training, the knowledge, and the wisdom we need in our own lives to stay one step ahead on the learning curve of those He desires for us to disciple. Then let us ask God earnestly to bring us to those He knows have ready hearts and those who will "fit" with the particular passion and personality He has placed within each of us. God can pair people perfectly in pairs, in groups, in congregations. He desires to fulfill in us the very thing He has called us to do—to go and make disciples. His hand is not short. May His name be glorified!

Legacy IS WHAT WE LEAVE INVESTED IN OTHERS

A HARVEST OF SOULS

requires a legacy of DISCIPLESHIP

A Harvest of Souls

2019 Theme Statement

Worship in Awe and Wonder

Visual for 2019 Goals

My fourth painting was a reflection of my 2019 theme statement. I was encouraged to write out goals for the year in an early 2019 message. I sat with my journal in front of me asking the Lord what was important to Him. One theme resounded louder than all the goals that were later numbered down my journal page. Worship in awe and wonder! As the Holy Spirit led me into worship throughout the year, this theme only intensified. By the time I painted this picture a little over a year later, I had come to know worship as the highest form of prayer and the highest calling of human beings. It is indeed our eternal occupation as sons and daughters of the King.

Dr. David Holt gave a message on worship one Sunday morning shortly after I began attending Living Hope Church. He said worship attracts the presence of God. It lifts the human spirit. It unites the body of Christ, and it dispels the enemy. That message touched a chord in my heart that began to play the melody of worship to my King. Prior to experiencing worship from this place deep in my heart, I had worked hard, prayed hard, given generously, and even fellowshipped well. I had loved sincerely and tried to demonstrate that love by hard work and faithful service, but I was stifled in my worship and straitjacketed into lifelessness. Something was missing in my own heart as I went through the motions of worship. But when God began to open my spirit to real worship, His Spirit brought new life to me. God was doing a great work in me. He was breaking the chains that bound me, the chains of rule-based and performance-based religion, the chains of maintaining the right outward appearance and legalism, and the chains of comparison. He was beginning a process in me that was going to take time, but He was giving me His victory over the enemy one battle at the time.

So much in my relationship with God had been so good that it made it hard for me to define what was lacking, yet I knew there was something missing in me that was never quite definable. I had a desire to serve God, and I tried hard to fulfill my roles and be a good Christian and a good church member. Drained, lifeless, tired, and weighed-down characterized even my best efforts at Christianity and serving God before I tasted the life-giving experience of worshiping God in Spirit and in truth. But when real worship came and I began to worship freely in the Spirit, His life began to flow into me, and it charged my spiritual batteries with the power of the Holy Spirit. God was breaking me free from the sense of lethargy, tiredness, legalism, and traditions. God had put me in a place where the life-giving pulse of the Spirit of God was palpable. In this place God had raised up a body alive with life, passion, praise, and worship.

Psalm 7:17
I will praise the Lord
according to His righteousness:
and will sing praise
to the name
of the Lord Most High.

Psalm 9:1–2
I will praise Thee, O Lord,
with my whole heart;
I will show forth
all Thy marvelous works.
I will be glad and rejoice in Thee:
I will sing praise to Thy name,
O Thou most High.

Worship in awe and wonder!

God the Father, God the Son, and God the Holy Spirit

The Trinity

My fifth painting came as a result of a desire to have a visual to use to teach my grandchildren about the Trinity. Meeting the Holy Spirit in relationship and understanding and receiving wonderful gifts of the Spirit revealed a new place of serving within the body of Christ to me. No longer did I muster up the strength to serve because serving was the right thing to do. I began to serve out of a flow of God's Spirit coming from within me, from His filling and anointing on my life. I began to serve Him from a heart of worship.

Speak to Me

I painted the sixth picture during a time I was just relaxing in the presence of the Lord. I had no theme and no agenda. I just painted for the sheer enjoyment of painting. But then a picture from a much earlier journal entry came back to my heart, and the words to another song formed in my heart as I sang my prayer to the Lord. Later I repainted the scene to add to the original picture what had been in my heart.

The Father's Voice

Speak to Me, Oh Lord

This seventh picture was the scene Jesus had showed me in my heart. I was in a field of yellow flowers and beautiful green grass. Above me was a beautiful blue sky with white fluffy clouds. But the most beautiful part was I was not alone in that beautiful place. I was there twirling in the sunshine, and Jesus was there with me. His laughter was the music in the wind. Speak to me, Oh Lord!

Speak to Me, Oh Lord

I want to hear Your voice to me in the darkest of the night
I want to hear Your voice to me in the brightest of the light
Speak to me, speak to me, Oh Lord

I want to walk beside You in the deepest valley place
I want to walk beside You in the highest mountain space
Walk with me, walk with me, Oh Lord

I want to gaze upon You when I cannot see Your face
I want to gaze upon You when You reveal Yourself in grace
Show me You, show me You, Oh Lord

I want to praise and worship when the song in me has died
I want to praise and worship when the song is bursting forth inside
Sing to me, sing to me, Oh Lord

I want to praise and worship when there's no song inside
I want to praise and worship when in You my heart confides
Sing to me, sing to me, Oh Lord

So, Father, keep my eyes on You no matter what comes my way
And the joy that lives inside of me comes bursting forth as praise
And I love You, Lord, and I praise Your name
And I give You all my praise
For You are God, You're still the same
You are God of all the earth
And I sing, Oh Lord, for I cannot be
I cannot be silent
And the joy in me is a never-ending song
And I'll praise Your name as the day is long

Time and Eternity

Hebrews 13:5
...for He hath said,
I will never leave thee,
nor forsake thee.

This painting is my favorite just because of what it means to me. It grew out of a journal entry that has deeply encouraged my heart over and over. That journal entry, from May 9, 2019, is as follows:

"My daughter, I will not leave you. I will not. Moving from one time and season to the next does not remove you from My presence or take you further from Me. I will not take away from you our fellowship just because your life is changing. Remember, I see your life already complete—the whole picture already done. When I say I know the plans I have for you, I know them from a completed view. You live in hope and faith looking forward into time and life. I live in existence and completeness outside the realm of time. See the picture I am showing you of a person walking through a measured journey. All that is behind him is laid out in clear pictures of what has taken place—like frames on a piece of film. What is before him is a measured line with frames that are covered by an opaque fog shrouding the frames from view by the human eye. Yet, I see every frame and the length of the line as well. Walk forward in faith. Do not be afraid of the frames still before you just because they are shrouded in the unknown. See the picture I am giving you now of you walking in that line of frames and Jesus there with you holding your hand? You turned and looked behind you and saw Jesus in every past frame holding your hand." This was my response back to Him: "Thank You, Father. My tears right now are from gratefulness for You and for Jesus and the Holy Spirit. ...I step into the next frame by faith, holding Jesus's hand. I can't see a thing, but I can feel His hand holding mine. I purpose to walk by faith, listening every moment for Your voice. I lay it all down before You. I surrender everything to You."

Time and Eternity

Wings Like an Eagle

These next two paintings came from my journal entry of April 24, 2018. I was just beginning to really experience what it means as a daughter of the King to hear my Abba Father's voice to me. Because of ingrained ways of thinking and ways of believing from my past, this developing experience of hearing my Father's voice to me was very new and very fragile. In raw honesty and transparency, I share here what I had written then.

"So much is beginning to come together, and yet at a moment's whisper it could all slip from me because I don't quite grasp it yet in a way that fully holds it as mine. I know I am beginning to see and to hear, and then those moments come that I doubt and even ridicule myself for believing this could be true. But I push the doubts away because I know my Savior's voice. I know it is real!"

I then went on to make a list of the hurdles I still needed to take to the Lord and work through. Looking back over the list, I realized they were all ingrained ways of thinking that were false or partially false. I journaled again.

"All these things contained an element of truth, but so much was missing. Now I am having to relearn how to visualize, how to hear, how to remember what I dream and seek the meaning from the Lord. And in doing all that, Scripture itself is becoming alive with God's voice to me. I am hearing Him in rhema words like never before."

I had "turned off" so much in my brain and suppressed most right brain functions in the areas of expression—art, music, visualization, and more. These suppressed areas had directly affected my ability to hear God's voice to me in an intimate, conversational way. I continued writing my thoughts before the Lord.

"I have over the course of time shut down my desire to create pictures with pastels and much of the other creative side in me because I believed it stole time from what I should be doing. I never had musical training and can't sing or play any musical instrument, yet music is in my heart and soul. I have known that for a long time. I have pages of poems and words to songs stuffed away in a notebook, and yet my inner being begs for music and for worship as if it has been starved for years.

I am like a caterpillar that crawled into a cocoon—a world of walls and rules and lists and safety—now afraid to come out, afraid that wings are somehow wrong. But the threads are unwinding and at the right time God will give me wings. He will give me wings like an eagle, and I will soar to new heights with Him. There is a tremor of excitement and anticipation for what is to come."

Though I painted these pictures almost a year after writing that journal entry, the excitement in my heart for what the Lord has done, is doing now, and will do in my future is still just as fresh as it was the day those words were penned. My love for worship has only intensified, and my gratitude for my Savior grows deeper day by day. I am a daughter of the King of kings, a bride in love with her Bridegroom and Savior, a wife, a mother, a daughter, a grandmother, a sister, a friend—all forgiven, set free, made whole, made righteous, sanctified, set part, made holy, loved, called by name, and sung over by the King of kings.

Isaiah 40:31

But they that wait upon the Lord shall renew their strength; they shall mount up with wings as eagles; they shall run, and not be weary; and they shall walk, and not faint.

A Tribute to My Father

My wise and loving Father
Made us just the way we are
He knew us and He loved us
And planned the lives that
would be ours

He did the thing He needed to
To bring glory to His name
And though it's hard to understand
It's for God's glory and His fame

The things that are beyond us
The things we cannot understand
These are the things we must accept
From His wise and loving hand

The things that bring us pain
Are the things that shape and mold us
They take us to a special place
Of surrender and sweet trust

For the pain is His knife
That cuts the self away
It does the work that He desires
To make us ready for that Day

For now abide and trust
Until He gives us sight
Then we'll understand His reasons
And the darkness will be light

The answers that we've longed for
Will be revealed to us that day
And when we come to
understand them
All glory to Him, we'll say

My Father, I choose to trust You
Though as yet I cannot see
The outcome of Your plan
That You've designed for me

A. Patterson 7-24-05

Threads Unwinding

Wings Like an Eagle

Isaiah 61

Trees of Righteousness

Isaiah 61:3

...to give unto them beauty for ashes,
the oil of joy for mourning,
the garment of praise for the spirit of
heaviness;
that they might be called trees of
righteousness,
the planting of the Lord,
that He might be glorified.

Slowly I began to find more and more freedom
in worship and in my expression of my worship to the Lord. I lost count of my paintings and began to give some of them away, though I was quite surprised, well, shocked really, that anyone would want one. I remember someone asking me what I was going to do with all of them and, embarrassed, I replied, "I don't know. I could paint over them, I guess." Imagine my surprise when someone asked me to paint a tree for a letterhead emblem.

Letterhead Emblem

Victory

Planted by the Rivers of Water

This painting was one of the choices for the letterhead emblem. After the other painting was chosen, I took this one as my own book cover design and reminder of Christ's victory in my own life if I abide in Him and He in me.

His righteousness is not anything that I can earn but a gift that I must accept by faith. Derek Prince said that God will not do anything for us until He has first made us righteous. He said it is the first thing God does when we approach Him.

Psalm 1

Blessed is the man that walketh not in the counsel of the ungodly,
nor standeth in the way of sinners, nor sitteth in the seat of the scornful.
But his delight is in the law of the Lord;
and in His law doth he meditate day and night.
And he shall be like a tree planted by the rivers of water, that bringeth forth his fruit
in his season; his leaf also shall not wither; and whatsoever he doeth shall prosper.
The ungodly are not so: but are like the chaff which the wind driveth away.
Therefore the ungodly shall not stand in the judgment,
nor sinners in the congregation of the righteous.
For the Lord knoweth the way of the righteous:
but the way of the ungodly shall perish.

Abiding Under the Shadow of the Almighty

Psalm 91:1

He that dwelleth in the secret place
of the most High shall abide
under the shadow of the Almighty.

A growing theme in my life was depicted by the phrase *abiding under the shadow of the Almighty*. The Lord planted a seed thought in my heart of writing a book by that title and sharing my journey of learning to hear His voice to me. A short time after painting this picture, a dear couple prayed for me and prayed that the Lord would hide me under the shadow of the cross. They had no idea that I had recently painted this picture, but their prayer confirmed what God was speaking to my heart. I purposed then to obey, and that book is now in process.

In the Shadow of the Cross

Clothed in Christ's Righteousness

This painting illustrates the picture that formed in my heart the day after I wrote the words to the following poem. Too many times I had heard the internal accusations, the enemy's taunts and accusations against me, telling me that I was not worthy, that I had no value and no worth. Jesus, my Savior, stood between me and the enemy with His hand outstretched and His eyes fixed on God the Father. His authoritative voice resounded with the words "not guilty" as He wrapped me in His robe of righteousness.

A Thousand Songs

The enemy comes and calls my name
Condemning me in guilt and shame
He mockingly accuses me
He tells me lies and crushes me

But I call out to my Father above
And He responds in grace and love
He hears my cry and calls my name
I run to Him; He's still the same

A God of love rescues from sin
With open arms He draws me in
I run to Him and behold His face
And I fall there in His embrace

His heart beats there next to mine
Love flows out and gives me life
And here I rest in this place I find
Peace from all the war and strife

He pulls me in close by His side
He whispers truth where the enemy lied
I lean in hard to hear His voice
I choose Him now; He is my choice

And I believe the truth proclaimed
I will not hear the enemy
I stand alone in Jesus's name
The enemy has no hold on me

I worship You, Oh God, my King
You are the One that makes me sing
I lift my voice to You alone
Oh, Holy One upon Your throne

I sing to You the songs of love
I hear You now Holy One above
I raise my voice to proclaim Your name
To lift You high in holy fame

And You whisper back Your love for me
Till it echoes through my destiny
I hear Your voice like thunder now
A daddy's love in booming sound

I feel Your hand surrounding me
Like a shield protecting me
And the enemy, he has to flee
He can no longer accuse me

So here I stand by faith alone
Resting in You till You call me home
And I look up into the sky
Waiting to hear that trumpet nigh

I'll see Your face,
Your arms outstretched
Coming for me till I am fetched
I rise to meet You in the air

Clothed in Christ's Righteousness

Worthy is the Lamb

Revelation 5:12
Worthy is the Lamb that was slain
to receive power, and riches,
and wisdom, and strength, and honor,
and glory, and blessing.

This painting came out of a time of private, personal, and intense worship. I never intended to share it because it did not do justice to the desire that was within my heart. But even in its childish and simplistic form, it was still worship from my heart. My heart yearned to touch the very throne room of God as song went forth from my lips. The song was just as childish and simplistic as the painting, but I have to believe that even the angels were singing.

The Sound of Angel Music

Oh I hear the sound of angel music playing in my ears
It is sweet and beautiful

It proclaims my Savior's holy name so high and lifted up
It is so magnificent

So I lift my voice in song and praise and proclaim my God is good
He is high and lifted up

My heart cries holy, holy, holy, holy is the Lord
Oh, He lives eternally

And I've found a place to rest my hope in the promises of God
They'll stand firm eternally

And I've found a place to build my faith on God's unchanging Word
It is true and right and just

And as I look back upon His Words, the record stands the test
It will never, never fail

And as I look back upon my past, I see His loving hand
Full of grace and truth and love

So I can live my here and now according to His Word
For it will never, never fail

And I've learned to hear His voice to me; He whispers in my ear
Words of life, comfort, and hope

And my heart is thrilled as I lift my eyes and gaze upon His face
There He reigns in awesome power

And I cannot know the mystery of His never-ending love
It is deep and wide and full

For my God above reached down in love and drew me to Himself
Yet He was high and lifted up

And I found within His arms of love a place of grace and rest
It is sweet and beautiful

(Written 9-29-19)

He is Worthy

Only in the Crushing

Daily Communion

This painting came after listening to a Sunday morning message that spoke one point vividly to my heart—"All things for His glory and my good." Then the phrase "only in the crushing" began to repeat over and over in my mind. Another point made in that message was the importance of taking communion daily. My heart became overwhelmed with the goodness of God—even in the crushing because it is in the crushing that the flow of His Spirit comes. His Spirit flows in the crushing, and then communion, daily communion, brings His anointing, His power, His presence—all so real and so present.

This sermon struck a chord in my heart. As I kept thinking about how God uses the hard things for good, I saw a picture of grapes in my mind. I shared these thoughts with my small group that Sunday evening, and afterward painted this picture. Then after the first picture of the grapes and the bread, I painted numerous pictures on scraps of wood. I could not get enough of what those grapes and the bread really symbolized. The gratification in painting something as simple as a bunch of grapes and some bread was surprising even to me. I painted on anything I could find. The original *Daily Communion* painting was on a piece of an old door I had removed from a barn we have on our property. As I gave some of these bread and grapes paintings away, I lost track of their numbering; but painting them brought me great joy and a deep sense of gratitude to my Savior.

Only in the Crushing

His Blood Shed for Me

The Bread and the Wine of Communion on Canvas

Always Enough

Gratitude

Luke 22:19
This is My body
which is given
for you:
do this
in remembrance
of Me.

For My Good and for His Glory

For His Glory

All Things for Our Good and His Glory

Creativity

What Is in My Hand?

Happy Birthday

This painting was done on a scrap of wood to hold up as a birthday sign during a Zoom meeting for a little girl celebrating a birthday during the COVID-19 quarantine. The more that I grew in worship and communion with God, the more I was filled and stirred up by the Holy Spirit, and the more creativity seemed to flow.

A question began to stir in my heart. "What is in your hand?" How can I use what is in my hand right at the time a need presents itself? God always provides for the things He desires for us to do. My own reasoning wanted to argue, "It's not good enough." But the joy of obedience overrides the arguments of human reasoning. How many opportunities have I missed because I listened to my own reasoning or my own fears and inadequacies instead of listening to the voice of the Holy Spirit, even in something as simple as painting a birthday sign because that is what I had in my hand at the time.

Unsearchable Treasures of God

Psalm 145:3
Great is the Lord,
and greatly to be praised;
and His greatness is unsearchable.

The next three paintings came after listening
to a Sunday morning message that spoke of God's attributes being so vast that we will never understand them all completely. Yet there are also aspects of His character that are easy enough for children to grasp. In my mind I sensed the vast treasures and unsearchable riches of God, yet He is our Abba Father with a heart of love for His children—love as vast as the ocean.

Water on Dry Ground

You've poured out Your Spirit, Lord
Like water on dry ground
You've called me Your treasure
And loved me beyond measure

Like rain on a summer day
You've washed all my sins away
Your promises to me are true
They're faithful like morning dew

You've promised to keep me
To keep me from falling
I hear Your voice to me, Oh Lord
To me it is calling

You've promised to hold me
To love me forever
I'll trust You with all my heart
You'll leave me, Oh never!

So I love You, Lord
I worship You and praise You forever
You are mine and I am Yours
And nothing will sever

Your promises are true, Lord
They're faithful and true, Lord
And I will obey You, Lord
And love You forever

So like water on dry ground
I receive Your Spirit
Oh fill me now to capacity
And speak, let me hear it

Hallelujah, hallelujah
Ha..ha..lle..lu..jah
I worship You and praise You
And praise You forever

(Written 11-15-19)

Unsearchable Treasures of God

Vast as the Ocean

Attributes of God

Spiritual Warfare

Piercing the Darkness Through Prayer

This painting was the result of several things coming together simultaneously. God had been speaking to my heart on the power of prayer and how it shifts things in the unseen realm. The awareness of the darkness invading the world and yet the availability of multitudes of heavenly hosts to war on our behalf, if we but ask in prayer, was forefront in my thoughts. I had recently read a few chapters of Frank Peretti's book *This Present Darkness* to my son and his girlfriend after I picked up a *Decision* magazine with a picture of a man praying on the front cover. In my mind's eye, the picture was of my youngest son praying transposed over that picture on the magazine. However, there was a major difference in the two pictures. The picture I saw contained not only the forces of evil surrounding the one praying but also the angelic forces sent out in response to the prayer of that beloved child of God.

Our children might not realize the power of prayer, especially if they are not walking closely with the Lord and communing with Him daily in conversational prayer. They may not realize the power of prayer if they have been raised in a legalist religious home environment where being good meant doing all the right things and checking them off each day and prayer was only one more thing on the list.

Over the last several years, God has changed my life and put me in relationship with Him and given me the precious treasure of two-way conversational prayer with Him. I have attempted to share with my children the difference this has made in my life, in my prayers, and in my relationship with God the Father, God the Son, and God the Holy Spirit. Oh, the precious, wonderful Holy Spirit that prays for us and through us and with us!

So I felt the Lord leading me to paint the picture and put my son in the picture as the child of God kneeling in prayer. I then showed him the painting and asked him if he wanted it. "Yes," he responded. "It's a little creepy, but I'll take it." It now resides in his room as a reminder that the unseen is more real than the seen and the power of prayer shifts things in the unseen world and calls into motions multitudes of God's warring angels. Yes, the unseen realm of evil is creepy, but it is very real, and we are more than conquerors in Christ Jesus our Lord. We overcome by the blood of the Lamb and the word of our testimony. We can do all things through Christ who strengthens us. No weapon formed against us shall prosper, and ultimately the battle is the Lord's!

2 Corinthians 10:4

For the weapons of our warfare
are not carnal,
but mighty through God
to the pulling down of strong holds.

Piercing the Darkness Through Prayer

A. Patte

The Battle is the Lord's

Oh, Satan cannot win this war
The battle is the Lord's
Jesus Christ is King of kings
He's Lord of all the earth

Yes, Jesus Christ is Lord of lords
He's God of all the earth
I lift my voice to Him I'll sing
I'll praise His holy name

And to my King my voice will ring
And I'll proclaim His fame
No, Satan cannot win this war
The battle is the Lord's

For Jesus Christ is King of kings
He's Lord of all the earth
So I will praise and worship Him
I'll lift my hands in praise

No, Satan cannot win this war
The battle is the Lord's
Satan's a defeated foe
His end is sealed I know

So Holy Spirit come and fill
And fill our hearts with every praise
We worship now before the throne
We'll sing for all our days

Your Spirit, Lord, is raining down
It's raining down in love
Streams of mercy and of grace
Cascading from above

We love You Father, Holy One
We love You, Jesus Christ
We love You, Spirit, three in One
The Holy Trinity

No, Satan cannot win this war
The battle is the Lord's
Satan's a defeated foe
His end is sealed I know

So, Holy Spirit come and fill
And fill our hearts with every praise
We worship now before the throne
We'll sing for all our days

Your Spirit, Lord, is raining down
It's raining down in love
Streams of mercy and of grace
Cascading from above

We love You Father, Holy One
We love You, Jesus Christ
We love You, Spirit, three in One
The Holy Trinity

The Night Cometh

John 9:4

I must work the works
of Him that sent Me while it is day.
The night cometh
when no man can work.

May we be like trees planted by the rivers of water bringing forth our fruit in this season now, for the time is short and the days are evil and the night draws very near. Let our fruit be the fruit that comes only from the filling and overflowing of the Holy Spirit stirred up within us. Let it be the fruit that is produced only by abiding as a branch drawing life and sustenance from the trunk rooted down deep in the eternal Word that is life itself. Let Word and Water be combined in us to produce the strength to stand. Let that fruit that is produced in us be His love manifested as joy, peace, patience, kindness, goodness, and self-control. Let that fruit be the fruit of winning souls into the Kingdom (see Psalms 1).

May we be trees of righteousness causing those who mourn to be glad, giving beauty for ashes and the garment of praise for the spirit of heaviness as we share the truth of God's Word and the blessed hope of the Gospel that the Lord may be glorified (see Isaiah 61:3). May we go out with joy and be led forth with peace. May the mountains and the hills break forth before us into singing. May all the trees of the field clap their hands as we offer thanksgiving, praise, and worship to our King. May we bring something to Him as He has brought everything to us. And as we praise and worship, may the earth quake and prisoners be released. May the powers of darkness tremble in their places and flee away into the night (see Isaiah 55:12).

May we be as a tree planted by the waters that spreads out her roots by the river. May our leaves be green with His life and vitality. May we not wither in the heat that is to come nor be afraid in the year of drought. May we never cease to bear fruit. And regardless of how dark the night, how dry the season, how hot the heat, may we flourish beside the river of life (see Jeremiah 17:8).

May our light shine the brightest in the darkness of the night. Though this earth grows strangely dim, may we look up and find that our redemption draws very near. And as we wait and watch in the darkness descending around us, may we occupy until He comes and be found faithful at our post. May our lives bear fruit here and now. May we not delay for the night cometh when no man can work (see John 9:4).

The Night Cometh

A Mighty River

A Mighty River

A Patterson

John 3:8

The wind bloweth where it listeth,
and thou hearest the sound thereof,
but canst not tell whence it cometh,
and whither it goeth:
so is every one that is born
of the Spirit..

On November 10, 2020, I began my day like any other spending time with my God and my Savior. I picked up my pen and waited to hear His voice, as is my custom after I have poured out my heart to Him in prayer. The following words are part of what I believe He spoke to my heart as I paused in quietness to listen to Him.

"My daughter, I desire to glorify My name in all the earth. You will not always understand My methods or My timing. Time is not an issue to Me because My plan will be accomplished, and I will glorify My name. Dear one, you see today and yesterday. You see minutes and moments. I see tomorrow. I see eternity. So in My vision you can find rest, strength, stability, hope, courage, and endurance. "To the end" means a part of My plan inserted into a container of time. Faith is to remain steadfast until that container is full. Now rise up in spiritual vision above the realm of time and look with Me at the whole plan completed. See, I gave you a glimpse, an aerial view, of My plan for all the ages; but see the end. The end is just the beginning, the beginning of a blessed eternity of holiness and justice. Do not fret or despair. Deception and injustice will not prevail. My holiness is prevailing and will prevail. Worship now in the beauty of holiness.

It is My holiness that I desire in you, for My holiness makes beautiful. The King greatly desires your beauty when your beauty is the beauty of My holiness. That is what I desire for you in this day, that you be clothed in the garments of praise and made beautiful in My holiness. Bring Me gifts and sacrifices of praise and thanksgiving. Bow before Me in worship, and I will reveal My glory to you in measure. My glory will invade your heart and give you a new heart. My glory transforms, renews, makes new, purges out, washes whiter than snow, separates, sanctifies, and sets apart all that it touches. My glory shines in the cross, in the blood, in My Son, in His death, in His burial, in His resurrection, in His ascension, in His return, in His reign, in His Kingdom, in His Kingship, in His roar, in His judgment, and in His justice. My glory shines forth in My Spirit, the seven Spirits of God—not divided but unified in My body the church. My glory goes forth in My Spirit to all who will receive.

Receive, dear one, receive more of My Spirit. I will cause My Spirit to flow into you so fully that your life will become a flowing river of life full of My Spirit. Now the source must be continual to live as a river. I offer you this flow. To live as a river means you are a channel only. Are you willing to become a channel only? That means you will not choose the direction nor force of the flow. That means the water will wash away the things you might desire to hold on to. That means the harder the force of the flow, the more fully it flows out to others, but it also means the harder the force of the flow, the more intense becomes the wearing away of rough places.

Daughter, I set two choices before you this day. I give you a choice between right and right. I will be with you in either choice. You may live quiet and tucked away as a calm shallow lake with a trickling stream to flow into you. Others will come and enjoy the lake and taste the devotional goodness of a trickling stream. Your life will touch only those closest to you, and I will raise up another to live as a mighty flowing river. Or you may choose to experience Me as a mighty flood, a flowing river, a cascading torrent of power and presence. You may choose to live as a channel for the flow of My Spirit as a mighty river. This choice will cost more than living tucked away in the calm place of a shallow lake with a trickling stream, but your life will touch thousands and I will be with you still. I will not shame you for the choice you make, but I am offering you this day, this moment, the privilege of stepping into My plan for the ages. Nothing will be the same, BUT I will never change.

I AM the same yesterday, today, and forever. I will be with you to the end, and the end is the beginning.

You asked Me what I desired to do today. My answer is that I desire to flow through your life like a mighty river. I desire to fill you and flood you with My Spirit. I desire for your life to be a channel to reach thousands upon thousands for the end is soon to come and that is the beginning. I desire for you to lay down all that you call yours and be made fully Mine. When you are fully Mine, I will be fully yours. There is no loss greater than the gain of being fully Mine when I am fully yours. Daughter, the rewards of living as a mighty river will far outweigh the cost. I love you, dear one. I preserved your life at birth when the enemy asked to take it. I put My hand upon you. I kept you, and now the time has come. Will you be fully Mine?"

And my answer was, "Yes, Lord. Here I am. Use me. I want Your Spirit in fullest measure. Flow into me even now. I surrender myself to You fully and completely..."

Psalm 45:11
So shall the king greatly desire
thy beauty:
for He is thy Lord;
and worship thou Him.

Jeremiah 29:13–14
And ye shall seek Me,
and find Me,
when ye search for Me
with all your heart.
And I will be found of you,
saith the Lord...

Proverbs 8:17
I love them that love Me;
and those that seek Me early
shall find Me.

2 Chronicles 16:9
For the eyes of the Lord
run to and fro
throughout the whole earth,
to show Himself strong
in the behalf of them
whose heart is perfect toward Him...

When God is Resting in the Middle of a Storm

Luke 8:23
But as they sailed He fell asleep...

The desire to paint this scene was born in my heart as I read to my granddaughters from a children's Bible storybook published by Christian Focus Publications. In the book I saw an illustration by Mackay Design Associates Ltd., and my mind immediately went back to the message on the sleeping God that I had heard about a year prior. My takeaway from the message, "God, You Did What?/The Sleeping God," by Dr. David Holt, Pastor of Living Hope Church, was if God is resting, then I can rest in His resting.

The message on the sleeping God was one of those key messages that unlocked a new door of understanding that I believe will profoundly impact the rest of my life. This message painted a picture in my soul not only of Jesus sleeping in a boat through a storm, but of God Himself resting.

Jesus being fully God and fully man slept that day, probably exhausted from teaching and ministering for extended periods of time before getting into that boat. But the God side of Him rested because His work was done for the moment. Back in Genesis, God rested on the seventh day—not because He was tired but because His work was complete. Jesus, in His humanness, so fully relied on the Father that His mind was able to lay aside the noise from the storm, the rocking and lurching of the boat, and the cold wet water from the waves spraying over His body. Through all this He was able to sleep in the middle of a storm. Was He that exhausted or was His reliance that deep? I believe His reliance was that deep. He KNEW (the intimate sense of knowing) His Father because He is One with His Father.

Now if I am a Christ follower then shouldn't I be following this example set by my Lord Himself—to rest through the storm? Funny, I always looked for the rest after the storm. So as I pondered the message from that Sunday, God gave me a beautiful picture with the eyes of my heart. God resting and me, His daughter, asking Him if I could come and snuggle up beside Him and rest with Him through my storm.

We all have storms and valleys—problems that seem to have no human answer, hard things that may have times of reprieve but never really a resolve. But these storms are the very place we find God. Ann Voskamp once said that gratitude follows grace in the same way that thunder follows lightning. She then goes on to call the storm itself grace, explaining that whatever drives us into God is actually a grace from God. She finishes by saying that there is no harvest without the storm. Yet I have begged and cried and pleaded with God to take away my storms, not realizing that the storm is actually a grace from Him. His answer has consistently been, "Be still and wait on Me." Many times He is not only in the storm, but He is the storm—wooing me to Himself. Thunder and lightning and cold wind cause me to beg Him to wrap me tighter in His robes of righteousness.

So last night in the middle of a storm, I cried out to Him again and here is His answer to me:

"My daughter, be strong in Me. Do not be afraid. I AM sovereign over every detail of your life. Do not be afraid of the storm. I am with you in the storm. Watch Me. If I am doing nothing then wait the storm out with Me. Do not fret or worry. If I am resting through the storm then rest in me. Let the waves roll and crash. Let the winds howl and the thunder roar. They cannot harm you even if I allow them to touch you. Fighting the wind and the waves won't stop them. Cowering in fear will not rescue you. If I am waiting to still the storm then wait with Me. You be still when the storm is not still. I will still the storm. I am in the storm and the storm is grace, and what drives you to Me is a grace from Me. Do not fear the battles in front of you. They are My battles. You will not need to fight them. I love you, daughter. Be still, My love."

And the words to the song "Raise A Hallelujah" (Bethel Music) kept ringing in my ears. *"I raise a hallelujah.... I'm gonna sing in the middle of the storm, louder and louder you're gonna hear my praises roar..."*

So instead of asking God to remove the storm, my prayer became, "Father, let the howling wind, the roaring thunder, and the crashing of the waves be the orchestra behind my voice as I raise my song in praise to You. And when the song is done, and I have worshipped You in faith, let me snuggle in beside You and rest in Your arms as You are resting even in the middle of the storm."

Matthew 11:28–29
Come unto Me, all ye that labour
and are heavy laden,
and I will give you rest.
Take My yoke upon you,
and learn of Me;
for I am meek and lowly in heart:
and ye shall find rest unto your souls.

Resting in the Middle of the Storm

Peace, Joy, and Love as Vast as the Ocean

Love as Vast as the Ocean

One day I will finish the other book, but for today I will just write what may be one chapter of that future book. Have you ever awakened to find your spirit soaring and your heart singing and the presence of God's Holy Spirit so real and so present that you thought your insides would just burst? Have you ever felt that the worship music playing in your head would lift you right up into the throne room itself? Has the desire inside you to be in God's presence and to hear His voice again in that moment been so strong that it was stronger than all your physical appetites? I think this must be what is called a spiritual high. I am pretty sure it is better than any high that could come from anything that we as humans try to use to lift our own spirits.

Or maybe you awakened to find the crushing weight of pain still sitting on your chest from the day before. Maybe the moment your eyes opened for a new day, the thoughts flooded in faster than you could process them. Maybe your heart was still crying from yesterday and the day before and the day before that. Maybe you just realized that your heart never stops crying. I have been there too, and if I get to pick which way to wake up in the morning, believe me, I am going to pick waking up to the spiritual high of God's presence and voice.

I think I hear you asking, "How do you do that? How do you choose which way to wake up each morning? Wouldn't we all stop our hearts from crying all the time if we could?" I used to think that the answer was found in fixing the things that caused the pain that made my heart cry in the first place. Discouragement and even despair descended as I realized that I cannot fix or change the things that cause the heart pain. Believe me I tried. I tried everything I knew to do, and when all that failed, I began trying everything I was counseled to do (within reason). Guess what? When all that failed, I came to the deepest place of brokenness. There was nothing else to try. Discouragement turned to hopelessness.

If I could hear your thoughts, I think they would be asking the silent question most people are too polite to ask. "What all did you try?" May I just go ahead and answer that for you? I tried being good. I tried doing all the right things for my situation, like reading my Bible, praying, being faithful in church, serving, adhering to certain guidelines of dress and speech and all that stuff. Since my situation is being a wife, I then tried being a very submissive, "godly" wife. I just *knew* I could win my husband that way without a word. I tried all of that for a very long time, thinking that I just needed to try harder and do a better job. As you probably already guessed, none of that worked to accomplish what

I wanted to accomplish. I wanted to stop the pain in my life. In fact, some of the things I tried made my circumstances worse—sometimes much worse!

You would have to know my story to fully understand this next attempt at stopping the pain in my life, but I'll just say that I had never really learned to hear God's voice to me personally. Yes, He did speak to me at times, but I did not hear Him clearly and conversationally. I was so unaware that this was even possible that many times I doubted what I did hear of His voice to me. I would be confident in the moment, but later doubt it or forget about it. My understanding had never been opened to the fact that God wants to have that kind of relationship with His children where we can talk to Him conversationally. So again, guess what happened next? Without being able to fully hear God's voice to me and to trust that what I did hear was truly His voice, I turned to others for advice and counsel. Let me just add, there is nothing wrong with getting godly, biblical advice and counsel, but it should never be in place of going to God first and listening to His voice.

Okay, I think you can guess how the scenario unfolded. I was very, very people dependent—especially spiritual leader dependent since I could not hear God for myself with confidence. I needed validation for everything and every decision. I was terrified of making the wrong decision. I was so desperate for answers, and I had already read, applied, and tried *everything* I knew to try. This brought me to the place of grasping for answers. I was sure someone had to have the answer and a better connection to the Lord than I did. Maybe I was not interpreting the Bible correctly. Maybe I was not trying hard enough. Maybe I did not know how to really pray correctly. All these thoughts went through my head. But it took failure in every area for me to finally realize that something was more seriously wrong than all of that. No matter what

I tried or whose advice I followed or how many programs I tried, there was no escaping the pain. The solutions were short-lived if they worked at all. One huge revelation came out of all the failure. No matter what I tried or what I did, I found every time that I was only trading one pain for another pain.

My brain had come up with its own way of coping with pain. Your heart can only cry for so long until it begins to harden over, stop feeling, and go numb. Forgetfulness fogs the past and dims the future. Funny jokes aren't really funny. Painful things don't really hurt quite as bad. Have you ever been there? You wake up one day and realize that you don't really laugh anymore. Odd that you still cry when the pain comes in deep, but, oh well, at least you don't cry as much. Yes, that is where I was too. But, oh wait, I am a Christian and that means I have the joy of the Lord, or at least I am supposed to. So you guessed it, this is where we learn to make ourselves smile and make ourselves laugh when someone says or does something funny. But one day that fails too. The party is over and your heart just goes back to crying; however, now it is a sob that comes from a broken heart. That broken heart has realized that there is no solution and no one that can help. This is the place of need, the place of brokenness, the place of laying everything down on the altar—not so that one can get what they want, but only because there is absolutely nothing else that can be done.

Here I was in this place of brokenness when God gently picked me up and put me in a place to show me something I had never seen before. I had to see it because I could not yet hear. He showed me a glimpse of worship, and something deep inside of me stirred. I felt the stirring but did not recognize what it was. How could I? I had never before experienced it. I felt this yearning deep, deep inside me, maybe it was even in that broken, numb place in my heart. I watched people around me worship God from their hearts. I was awed. Well, honestly, I was awed after I got over thinking they were weird. Maybe that is how much of a shell was wrapped around my heart in the beginning. But after the second or third exposure to people worshiping God from the heart, my heart was begging to know what this was that I was seeing. It wasn't just the music, though music can be an integral part of worship. It was like breathing air that was laden with worship. I could feel a sense of God's presence like I never had before.

I began asking myself—really, I was asking God, though I hadn't quite understood how to talk to Him conversationally yet—what was wrong with me. My thoughts said, "The same Jesus that died for them died for me. The same blood that was shed for them was shed for me. Why then am I a flat line? Why am I grateful for Jesus, yet, they are worshiping out of a heart of gratitude. What is wrong with me?" I turned those thoughts into a question directed toward God. And, oh, the story that unfolded after that. I have over twenty chapters already written for the future book that chronicles my journey of learning to hear God's voice to me. Learning to hear Him changed everything in my life. Yes, it was a process and it took time, but here I am today to share a resulting message of learning to live above pain in a beautiful relationship of worship.

To make a long story short, there was and is much comfort in hearing my Abba Father's voice to me. He gives me direction, comfort, correction, and so much more. I now know who I am as His daughter. I know that Jesus holds my hand and the Holy Spirit resides in me. I know that the Holy Spirit does more than just indwell me. He is stirred up within me day by day as I ask for His stirring up and His filling. I have learned to pray for the Holy Spirit to manifest Himself and flow out of me in every gifting He has put within me for His glory, for they are not my abilities and gifts. They are His outworking in me when I yield myself to Him. I have learned to listen to my Father's love song over me and to trust and believe in His great love for me. Yes, honestly, this one took a while. What I knew in doctrine and in my head about His love for me took a very long time to move the eighteen inches to my heart. But He is faithful, and eventually I did come to trust His love for me.

Trust and faith in God's love, which is an outworking of His grace, became the key that turned the lock on my heart and opened up the door for worship. Holy Spirit–led worship changed everything. Worship is the place of rest in the spirit, but it is also the place of ecstasy. Faith produces thanksgiving, and thanksgiving spills over into praise. These two combined take us right into the presence of God, and in God's presence the only thing we can do is fall down before Him in worship. Worship lifts us up above our circumstances, oh, and that means above the pain as well. Oops, I hear you balking at that last statement, so let me clarify. The pain is still there. You can still feel it. You may still cry at times because now your heart can feel again. However, there is a joy that comes only from worship that strengthens the heart in endurance and perseverance. If the pain was erased, there would be no need for endurance (bearing up under) and perseverance (not wiggling out from under). Yet, God calls us to endure and persevere, but He also makes a way. That way is through worship that comes only from being filled with His Spirit.

Worship is the highest form of prayer. Worship is also our eternal occupation and destiny. Think on that! Worship creates new neural pathways in our minds. It re-trains our thinking and re-focuses our gaze onto the One who holds all things in His hands, including the answers to our unfixable problems. His sovereignty becomes so big that our problems shrink back into a place small enough to fit into the palm of His hand. We stop seeing how big the giants in our lives are and start seeing how big God is. We begin to see how temporal everything in this life really is and how eternal our lives, after our lives on earth, really are. We begin to realize that for us as children of the King, this is all of hell that we will ever experience. This is as bad as it will ever get. But for unbelievers this is as much of heaven as they will ever experience. This is as good as it will ever get for them. Then we begin to find the good in every day in spite of the bad, the hard, and the painful.

In worship something else happens as well. We become more and more aware of God's presence and His voice. We become so consumed with who He is and what He is that our problems become even smaller in proportion to His hand. His glory begins to outshine the sun in our eyes. He becomes more and more, and everything else becomes less and less. We come to understand that our problems may never change while we live on this earth. We get to a place where we lay down the mind-set of thinking life is about being happy because we all deserve to be happy. We get to a place where life is no longer about our own plans and happiness. We realize that true happiness is really not happiness at all; it is joy that comes from the Holy Spirit being stirred up within us. That is when we have the most joy—when we are living out of His flow within us. That is when we rise up on the wind of the Spirit above the pain around us. We live in that place above the pain.

Will we still feel and cry? Absolutely! However, our tears become compassion for the other person—even the one who caused our pain or at least we thought they did. Our tears flow from a kind of grief that God feels in His own heart because He loves so deeply. They are no longer tears of feeling sorry for myself because "I have been hurt so badly and have no way to fix my problems." Pain then can even be beautiful.

Pain means we are alive and breathing and worshiping and feeling what our Father feels. Pain reminds us to pray and to intercede and to stand on God's Word declaring and decreeing what He says is true. Pain keeps us from being spiritual lepers having no feeling in our hands and feet, for it is our hands and feet that are to be the hands and feet of Jesus. Pain reminds us that someone else is hurting more than we are and reminds us to reach out in prayer and words and deeds of encouragement. Those words and deeds in turn become acts of worship, and worship lifts us up above the pain, and once again we find ourselves living above the pain.

Now let me also offer a word of warning. Living above the pain in a place of worship and hearing God's voice also paints a bright bull's-eye on our back—the only place we have no armor. Because of this we must be continually alert and continually stand facing the enemy head on. We must put on our armor daily through prayer.

Finally, as worship and intercessory prayer link hands, we rise above the pain and grief to live in a peace that passes all understanding. Joy overrides the grief even when tears fall. Tears for others, instead of our own griefs, become liquid worship that cause a sweet aroma before the Lord. Grief fuels intercessory prayer and praying in the Spirit with groanings that cannot be uttered. This type of praying moves the hand of God, inviting people to come out of the kingdom of darkness and into the Kingdom of Light as we labor and travail on their behalf. The end of laboring and travailing in pain is birth and great joy. That doesn't mean that everyone we fast and intercede for will turn to the Lord, because He will not override their free wills. He alone knows each heart. However, where there is an intercessor there is hope!

So on this day, rise up and intercede for those who cause you the deepest grief as you look in compassion at their lives. We have been given the greatest gift on earth, Emmanuel, God with us. Let us come and bow before Him. Let us worship Him and bring Him gifts. We bring the gift of tears, the gift of worship, the gift of intercessory prayer for others, the gift of ourselves offered as intercessors, as those willing to stand in the gap. But it is You, Jesus, that made our gifts possible. It is You, Holy Spirit, that lives through us to flow out of us into the lives of those around us. We love You, Lord; Father, Son, and Holy Spirit.

Matthew 1:23
...Emmanuel, which being interpreted is, God with us.

Gift Set for a New Friend

I have heard it said many times that you cannot out-give God. I know this is true from personal experience. The more I give away, it seems, the more is given to me. I gave painting number thirty-one away as a door prize at a ladies Christmas fellowship. One of the other ladies in attendance asked me if I ever sold my paintings. I told her I had only sold a few, and she said she wanted an ocean with a sunrise. I have been painting less than a year and am still in the learning phase, so I did not feel ready to paint for specific orders. I did, however, feel impressed by the Holy Spirit to go ahead and paint a picture for her showcasing the sky and the ocean. I decided to make it a little different from my previous ocean painting and paint it on two separate canvases and give it to this new friend as a framed set. I experienced sweet joy as I painted these in the quietness of a Christmas Day afternoon. The peace in my heart seemed to transfer onto the canvas, and the Holy Spirit unfolded a lesson on giving for me.

When we give because the Holy Spirit impresses our hearts to give, we are giving as unto the Lord. We are giving so that His name might be glorified as we bring joy to another in the body of Christ. In return, the giver is the one who gains the greater joy because what the giver receives is far greater than any financial gain. The giver receives peace, joy, and love as vast as the ocean. The giver gains the greatest blessing.

2 Corinthians 9:7
Every man according
as he purposeth in his heart,
so let him give;
not grudgingly, or of necessity:
for God liveth a cheerful giver.

Gift Set

He Parted the Water so I Could Walk Right through It

Parting the Red Sea

I was offered the opportunity to help lead a ladies' group, but there were several impossibilities in the way. I prayed and told the Lord I was willing to do it if He would make the way possible. I said, "Lord, You see the impossibilities. If You will part the waters of the Red Sea, the waters of impossibility, then I will walk through." I added one stipulation to my willingness. I said, "As long as Your Holy Spirit empowers me." In just a few weeks, God took care of the obstacles and made a way when there seemed to be no way. This picture is a memorial of His mighty hand. Every test of faith is ultimately to determine and reveal what we believe about God. He allows test to strengthen and refine our faith and to reveal things to us that we do not yet know about Him and His character.

11-29-20 Father, speak to me please. I am here before You now. The enemy has tried hard to distract me, but now I am here and quiet to listen to You.

> *"Dear daughter, I show you My heart in many ways. Even the seasons and nature around you whisper revelations about Me. Daughter, everything in your life comes back to what you believe about Me. Daughter, what do you believe about Me?"*

I believe You are good, very good. I believe that You love me and will not leave me. I believe that You are sovereign and holy and just. I believe that You have a purpose and plan and destiny for every believer. I believe I am to serve by leading a small group for ladies. I don't know the answer of when, how, where, and what time. Lead me. **Part the Red Sea (the sea of impossibility) and I will walk through it**. I believe.

12-04-20 *"Dear one, stand firm. I am with you. Be strong in Me and in the power of My might. I have heard your faith declared in your prayers. Now stand firm in those decrees. I love you, daughter."*

12-09-20 Father, the Red Seas in life are my tests of faith, aren't they? How do You want to speak to me in this? What do you want to say to me?

12-12-20 *"Daughter, I have divinely equipped you to stand in any and every battle. You lack no armor or ability to stand in My Spirit. Do not rely on human plans, schemes, or ideas to walk forward into the destiny I have set before you. Simply take each step in faith and by faith as it comes. Then you will step on to dry ground as I roll back the waters in front of you. You are mine! I am here for you."*

Exodus 14:16
But lift thou up thy rod,
and stretch out thine hand over
the sea, and divide it:
and the children of Israel
shall go on dry ground through
the midst of the sea.

The Oil of the Anointing

Matthew 25:4
But the wise took oil in their vessels...

I heard a statement somewhere that said something like the oil produced in the crushing becomes the oil of the anointing. The more I thought on this and the beauty of its message, the more a picture formed in my heart. Oil is symbolic of the Holy Spirit. Crushing symbolizes the tests of faith that we all experience. When we respond to these tests in believing faith and obedience to the Lord, the anointing power and presence of the Holy Spirit is released in our lives. We are made into vessels of honor as the fire of tests and trials purify our faith as gold tried in the fire. However, even the cracks and scars from our failures become a place where the anointing of the Holy Spirit spills out from our lives.

The Oil of the Anointing

Resting in the Storm

Over the course of time, I have come to find that the storms are indeed gifts of grace if I will lean into the storm instead of trying to outrun it or outmaneuver it. For it is in the storms, the valleys, the hard places, and the trials that I find the most fertile ground exists to bring about sanctification in me and a conformity into Christ's image. Christ's work in me is most often done in the hardest places. These places are where He has given me the songs, the poems, the pictures, and the prayers. Sometimes the hardness of our world is where we are changed into Christ's image, and as we are changed, we become world-changers. Father, may I be found resting in the storm.

Resting in the Storm

The Canvas of Our Lives

Romans 8:28

...all things work together for good
to them that love God...

God prompted my heart to paint this painting for a college-age friend of mine. She is young and beautiful and life should be beautiful too, but what happens when things do not go the way we hoped or expected? She unexpectedly found herself in a hard place through circumstances that were beyond her control. I painted this picture in stages to illustrate that sometimes the hard places in our lives are middle chapters that do not yet make sense in our limited viewpoint. It is only when the canvas is complete that we can see God's perfect plan. Until then we must look with the eyes of faith, trusting God to right everything that seems so wrong. I sent my sweet, college-age friend the pictures along with this text message:

I want to encourage you in something if I can.
Sometimes life seems to be going along pretty good.
Things are not perfect,
but they are good.
Then out of nowhere it seems
ugly marks are made across the canvas of our lives.
They seem out of place and purposeless.
They are painful,
and they seem to ruin the beauty
of what our lives were supposed to look like.
But if we trust our Father and wait on Him,
He will take those ugly marks
and make something beautiful in our lives.
Because of His perfect foreknowledge
He takes even what the enemy means for evil
and uses it to bring us into the exact destiny
He created each of us for.
Do not be anxious when even the ugly marks
of a loved one's addiction
seem to mar the canvas of your life.
God is writing your story.
He is painting your picture.
And He is creating something of great beauty in you!

The Canvas of Our Lives

Challenge

Finding Your Own Journey to Worship and Intimacy with God

There comes a time in most of our lives when we realize something is missing, for we all have a desire to worship something or someone. There is a God-shaped hole in our spirits that can only be filled with the intimacy of a conversational and relational relationship with God that goes far beyond knowing about God or knowing God from afar. This empty place leaves all of us longing, searching, and sometimes trying to fill that place with anything that can temporarily remove the loneliness and pain of a life outside of relationship with God and others.

The first step in beginning your own journey to worship and intimacy with God is entering into a personal relationship with Jesus Christ as Your Savior and Redeemer, for Jesus is the express image of God the Father. The Bible tells us that all have sinned and come short of God's glory and standard, but no one really needs to tell most of us that fact. Far too long we have lived trying to balance guilt with blame or trying to suppress shame that began before we could even write our own name. Most of us have lived with a voice of condemnation and unworthiness whispering incessantly in our ears. No, no one needed to tell us we were sinners with a sin problem and separated from God Almighty.

Some of us spent the majority of our lives trying to do better and be better. We held the silent assumption that the ache of something missing in our souls was our own fault because regardless of how hard we tried and how much we did, it was never enough. Some may have thrown in the towel and quit trying and just lived in the depths of depravity because the ache was there either way, and the effort of always trying to do better and be better was just too great. But here is where the good news comes in. The Bible not only tells us that we are all sinners; it clearly announces that God loved each of us so very, very much that He gave a remedy for our sins.

God, from before the beginning of time, had a plan for all the ages, and in this plan He chose to send His Son, Jesus Christ, to be the payment, the sacrifice, the Lamb that would take away the sins of the world. Jesus's willingness to come to earth and to be fully man, yet without any sin, while He was still fully God and live a perfect life, while being tempted in every way as we are, made Him the only one who could die in our place. You see, the Bible also tells us that the penalty of sin is death. Death means an eternal separation from God. So how does Jesus bridge that gap of separation for us? Jesus came to earth as a baby. We all know the Christmas story of the Christ-child born to Mary and placed in a manger and the shepherds coming to worship while the angels sang from above. But there is so much more to the Bible account of Jesus coming to earth. He lived a sinless life, being fully dependent on the Holy Spirit of God for everything He said or did. He could have simply lived out of His deity, but instead He lived fully out of dependence on the Father through the Holy Spirit. This means He suffered just as we suffer. He felt the same emotions that we feel. He got tired and felt the same temptation to be irritable just as we do. He got hungry. He needed time to rest and time to spend alone with His Heavenly Father just as we do. But in His humanness, He never sinned, not once.

He was rejected by many during His time on earth. He was mistreated and falsely accused. Here amidst the false accusations and the mistreatment is where He chose to lay down His own life in love and die for the sins of mankind. The Bible tells us that no man took His life from Him, but He chose to lay it down of His own accord. Sure, the people of that day thought they had taken His life in their animosity for Him. Satan and his kingdom also thought they took Jesus's life through the human agents of that day. They thought for a brief moment that they had won against God Almighty in the unseen war around us. But in reality, Jesus made the choice to die for all mankind. The Bible says that greater love hath no man than this, that a man lay down His life for His friends. Jesus laid down His life for us, all who would choose to accept Him and His free gift of salvation by faith. The Bible says that while we were yet sinners Christ died for us. He did this to reconcile us to God, to put us into right relationship with God, to give us His righteousness in place of our own filthy rags of trying harder to do better and to be better.

If we accept this free gift of salvation by faith in Christ alone in His finished work on the cross, we get salvation! Accepting Christ as Savior means turning away from our sins and self-effort in repentance. Repentance is changing the way we think. We were going one way, but then we turned in exactly the opposite direction in our thinking. We lay down our self-life and receive instead Christ's life in us and through us. Then He begins a work of sanctification inside of us. He changes us as we behold His glory. We no longer have to change ourselves in behavior modification and self-effort. We simply surrender to Him and allow Him to change us. It means letting go and letting Him work instead of holding on to our own efforts of goodness, and sometimes letting go hurts. It means laying down things that we have long held for security and identity, but we will find that the exchanges are more than worth it. We exchange our unbelief for His faith at the cross. We exchange our fear for His courage. We exchange our anxiety for His peace. We exchange our guilt and condemnation for His pardon. We exchange our shame for His glory. We exchange our unrighteousness for His righteousness. We exchange our anger for His meekness, and so much more. All these exchanges were made available to us at the cross of Calvary as free gifts if we will just receive what has been deposited in our spiritual bank account.

So what must we do to accept this free gift of salvation? The Bible tells us that we must simply believe in the Lord Jesus Christ, confessing Him with our mouths and acknowledging Him as Lord. Salvation is by faith and grace alone in Christ alone. We cannot earn it, and we will never deserve it. This is why it is the most beautiful gift we could ever receive. But salvation is only the beginning of this incredible journey with the Lord. As we come into an intimate and relational relationship with Him, communing with Him through worship and time in His presence, we are transformed. For it is in His presence that change takes place. Whether by time in His Word, by two-way prayer, by music, song, thanksgiving, and praise, by art, by dance, or by corporate worship with other believers, worship is the highest activity of mankind.

Where your own heart is stirred and you feel that yearning and that burning deep inside that comes with the stirring, that may be your place of worship. Enter fully into worship with your whole heart and soul. You do not need ability as much as you need availability and willingness to follow the Spirit. Do not be afraid to lift up your hands, to bow down on your knees, to shout hallelujah, to cry "Jesus, Jesus, Jesus," to lay prostrate before Him, to take up the paintbrush, to write out the songs, to sing out the music, to move in the dance of a pure and un-sensual movement as King David did, to play the instrument, to follow the Spirit however He moves in worship to our King! He is not looking for those who are the most gifted but those who are the most surrendered.

Prayer for becoming a follower of Christ and a worshiper of our great Triune God:

Father, I come to You this day as a sinner in need of a Savior. I know that I have fallen short of Your holiness and the standard of Your Word. I come helpless in myself to make myself any better. I confess my sins before You and repent of my old way of thinking. I turn now to You in wholehearted surrender asking for this free gift of salvation, which is Jesus taking my sin-debt and paying the penalty for my sins. I receive, in exchange for the penalty I deserved, life for all eternity with You. I ask for and receive not just the indwelling Holy Spirit in me, but a full filling and a stirring up of Your Holy Spirit in me. I want this filling and stirring day by day that I might worship You in the beauty of Your holiness. Thank You, Father!

Psalms 100

Make a joyful noise unto the Lord,
all ye lands.

Serve the Lord with gladness:
come before His presence with singing.

Know ye that the Lord He is God:
it is He that hath made us, and not we ourselves;
we are His people, and the sheep of His pasture.

Enter into His gates with thanksgiving,
and into His courts with praise:
be thankful unto Him, and bless His name.

For the Lord is good; His mercy is everlasting;
and His truth endureth to all generations.

Epilogue

I conclude this book a year and a half after beginning to paint for the very first time. After the initial draft was complete, I filed it away on my computer shortly after the last painting in this book was completed. Why did I stop with only a draft? I put it away because of the fears produced by my own inadequacies, lack of experience, lack of credentials, and the very amateur nature of my painting. Then I remembered the whole purpose of this book was to demonstrate how God can use the most insignificant members of His body to contribute to and be a significant part of the body as a whole as each member is submitted to and filled with His Holy Spirit. I went back through the files on my computer and found the written purpose of this coffee table book. I have included it here as a written reminder of why I would share this part of my journey with anyone who happened to pick up this book.

My goal in putting together a coffee table book is twofold. First, I hope to portray through this example the significance and beauty of small things and new beginnings as any believer learns to allow the Holy Spirit to flow through him or her in the gifts that God has put within them. I desire to demonstrate that worship comes in many forms and is not confined to a church pew and a hymn book, though it certainly occurs there too. Worship flows from the heart in the very areas that God has put as desires in each person's heart as we delight ourselves in Him. The more we ask for the Holy Spirit to stir us up, the more we will become aware of latent areas of our hearts awakening to His stirring. These are the areas He is equipping us to serve within the body of Christ to further His Kingdom. Not everyone is called to be a pastor or teacher, but we all have a place within the body. The body needs every member each with their own unique gifts and talents. It is up to us to join with the Holy Spirit and then use and develop these gifts. We will become more and more proficient with the use of each gift as He fills, stirs, and empowers us. This book is to demonstrate the discovery, the use, and the growing of precious gifts given by the Spirit no matter how insignificant these gifts may seem initially.

Second, I desire to portray part of my own personal journey in learning to hear God's voice and "see" the pictures He put within my heart to illustrate His words to me. I hope to portray through sharing even my most amateur and sometimes childlike paintings that God is not limited by my lack of ability. He only desires availability. The beauty is not in the paintings themselves but in the heart of communion with God. Intimacy with God is always beautiful! I hope to demonstrate how communication and intimacy grow when we start where we are by faith doing what we can with what we have, each time we feel the stirring of God's Spirit within us. If we are willing to obey no matter how small and how messy our attempts are, God will grow us in communication with Him and in effectiveness in the lives of others as we seek to serve Him by the power of His Spirit.

This coffee table book is a picture of how words and pictures grew within my own heart as I learned to communicate with God through two-way journaling and daily time in His Word. But words and pictures are only effective if we give away what we have received. Life comes when there is an inflow and an outflow. God is raising up an army for such a time as this. He is looking for those who will not be afraid to be humbled by their own inabilities but instead will count it a privilege to be available to be used by Him in the way He chooses. He is looking for those who will steward every gifting He has put within them by surrendering daily their time, their resources, and their talents to Him and His Kingdom. Oh, may we surrender all to Him and bow before Him in intimate worship!

Philippians 1:11

Being filled with the fruits
of righteousness,
which are by Jesus Christ,
unto the glory and praise of God.

John 10:27

My sheep hear My voice,
and I know them,
and they follow Me.

Psalm 29:2

Give unto the Lord the glory due
unto His name;
worship the Lord in the beauty
of holiness.

Psalm 96:9

O worship the Lord in the beauty
of holiness:
fear before Him, all the earth.

CPSIA information can be obtained
at www.ICGtesting.com
Printed in the USA
LVRC101611150322
713510LV00010B/185